SandCastle™

Baby
Australian Animals

It's a Baby
Koala!

Katherine Hengel

Consulting Editor, Diane Craig, M.A./Reading Specialist

ABDO
Publishing Company

Published by ABDO Publishing Company, 8000 West 78th Street, Edina, Minnesota 55439.

Copyright © 2010 by Abdo Consulting Group, Inc. International copyrights reserved in all countries.

Printed in the United States.

Editor: Liz Salzmann
Content Developer: Nancy Tuminelly
Cover and Interior Design and Production: Kelly Doudna, Mighty Media
Photo Credits: Peter Arnold Inc. (Gerard Lacz, Roland Seitre), Shutterstock

Library of Congress Cataloging-in-Publication Data

Hengel, Katherine.
  It's a baby koala! / Katherine Hengel.
    p. cm. -- (Baby Australian animals)
  ISBN 978-1-60453-577-8
  1. Koala--Infancy--Juvenile literature. I. Title.

  QL737.M384H46 2010
  599.2'5139--dc22
                                2008055076

SandCastle™ Level: Fluent

SandCastle™ books are created by a team of professional educators, reading specialists, and content developers around five essential components—phonemic awareness, phonics, vocabulary, text comprehension, and fluency—to assist young readers as they develop reading skills and strategies and increase their general knowledge. All books are written, reviewed, and leveled for guided reading, early reading intervention, and Accelerated Reader® programs for use in shared, guided, and independent reading and writing activities to support a balanced approach to literacy instruction. The SandCastle™ series has four levels that correspond to early literacy development. The levels are provided to help teachers and parents select appropriate books for young readers.

| **Emerging Readers** | **Beginning Readers** | **Transitional Readers** | **Fluent Readers** |
| (no flags) | (1 flag) | (2 flags) | (3 flags) |

SandCastle™ would like to hear from you. Please send us your comments and suggestions.
sandcastle@abdopublishing.com

Vital Statistics

for the Koala

BABY NAME
joey

NUMBER IN LITTER
1

WEIGHT AT BIRTH
$\frac{3}{100}$ ounce (less than 1 g)

AGE OF INDEPENDENCE
1 to 2 years

ADULT WEIGHT
11 to 31 pounds (5 to 14 kg)

LIFE EXPECTANCY
10 to 15 years

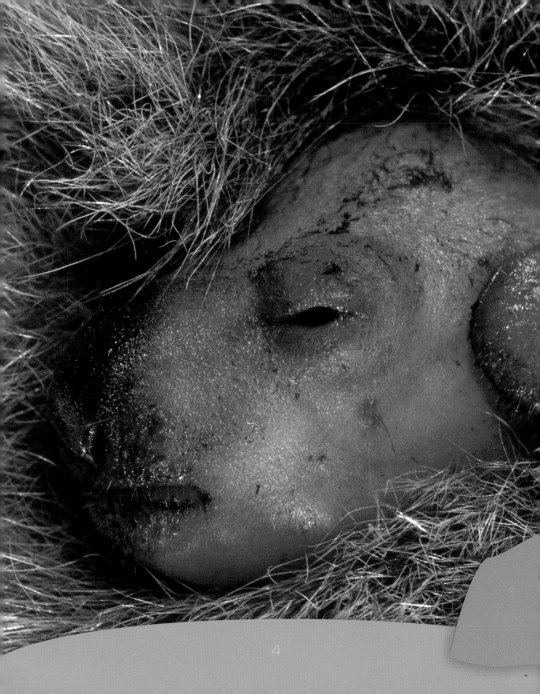

After a joey is born, it crawls into its mother's pouch. The joey uses its claws to hold onto its mother's fur.

Joeys are born **blind** and don't have ears or fur.

In the pouch, the joey **nurses** on its mother's milk. It also grows fur and becomes able to see and hear.

The joey stays in its mother's pouch for about six months.

When the joey leaves
the pouch, it rides
on its mother's back.

Koalas eat leaves from **eucalyptus** trees. They don't have to drink very much. They get water from the leaves they eat.

Koalas move slowly and sleep a lot. They sleep up to 18 hours a day!

Koalas are most **active** during the night.

13

A koala spends most of its life in trees. It only climbs down to move to a different tree.

Koalas have strong paws with long claws. Their paws have **opposable digits**. This helps them **grip** tree branches.

Koalas have **fingerprints** just like people do!

PLEASE DRIVE
CAREFULLY
WE LIVE
HERE TOO

The **main** dangers koalas face are dogs and being hit by cars.

A young koala stays with its mother for one to two years. Then it moves to its own tree.

Usually there is just one adult koala living in a tree.

Fun Fact

About the Koala

A koala eats about 1 pound (454 g) of **eucalyptus** leaves each day. That's about as much as five **salads**!

Glossary

active – moving around or doing something.

blind – not able to see.

eucalyptus – an Australian tree that is grown for its oil and wood.

fingerprint – the unique pattern of ridges in the skin on a fingertip.

grip – to hold onto.

independence – the state of no longer needing others to care for or support you.

main – usual or most common.

nurse – to drink milk from a mother's breast.

opposable digits – fingers or toes that can be pressed together to grip things. The thumb and fingers on a human hand are opposable.

salad – a mixture of raw vegetables usually served with a dressing.

To see a complete list of SandCastle™ books and other nonfiction titles from ABDO Publishing Company, visit **www.abdopublishing.com**.

8000 West 78th Street, Edina, MN 55439

800-800-1312 • 952-831-1632 fax